So there's going to be
a **new baby**
in your family?

And you'll soon be
a **big brother** or **big sister?**

Here's a special book just for **you**
to help you welcome
your **new baby.**

OTHER
MARLOR PRESS
BOOKS
FOR KIDS

Kid's Trip Diary

Kid's Squish Book

My Camp Book

Kid's Address & Writing Book

⭐ KID'S BOOK TO WELCOME A NEW BABY

FUN FOR A BIG BROTHER OR BIG SISTER

BARBARA J. COLLMAN

Foreword by

VICKI LANSKY

Published by

MARLOR PRESS

Saint Paul, MN

KID'S BOOK
TO WELCOME
A NEW BABY

Third Edition
Revised and Updated

Published by Marlor Press Inc.

Illustrations by Marlin Bree

Printed in the United States of America

ISBN 1-892147-00-9

Distributed to the book trade by
Independent Publishers Group, Chicago

MARLOR PRESS INC.
4304 Brigadoon Drive
Saint Paul, Minnesota 55126

CONTENTS

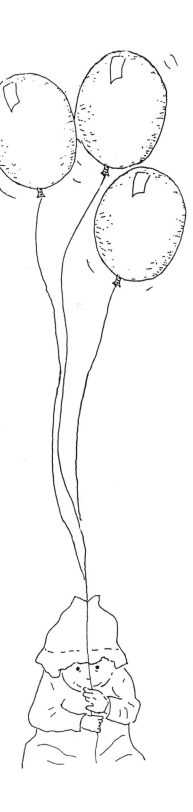

Part 4: WELCOMING THE NEW BABY

Part 5: WE GROW UP TOGETHER

Foreword

and a

special note

to parents:

SIBLING
PREPARATION

by VICKI LANSKY

The thought of having a new baby in the family can provoke an assortment of feelings in other children in the family. It may be fun to have a new brother or sister but it also raises lots of questions. You can help your child understand what it means to have a new family member and also help prepare for the arrival of this new sibling.

Your first child or children will wonder whether Mom and Dad still love them as much as ever. Feelings of insecurity may be aroused when preparation for the new baby begins to distract parents.

As the author of a number of best-selling books about parenting, I know that there are many things that can be done to help a child adjust. In my books, *Welcoming Your Second Baby* and *A New Baby at Koko Bear's House*, I discuss some of the ways parents can help an older child understand what to expect and give tips on ways to minimize their normal jealous feelings.

It is clear that Author Barbara J. Collman has thought about the needs of the older child. In this book, she has put together ideas and activities that will help a child to:

- boost her or his own self-esteem

- prepare for the baby's birth

- understand a baby's abilities and comprehension

- announce the arrival of the baby to friends and relatives

- appropriately entertain the baby

- help care for the baby

- and record some of the baby's milestones

All of these activities help to make an older child an important and cooperative family member.

Kid's Book to Welcome a New Baby doesn't guarantee there won't be any problems, but it will help a child adjust to this new family member.

Vicki Lansky is the author of many best-selling parenting books, including *Feed Me I'm Yours, Games Babies Play, Welcoming Your Second Baby* and *A New Baby at Koko Bear's House.*

KIDS !

How to have fun with this book

Something exciting is happening! Your family has told you that there will be a new baby in your home. You soon will have a baby brother or a baby sister! The *Kid's Book to Welcome a New Baby* will help you get ready to be a super big sister or big brother.

You can start today to read and do the activities in this book. You will learn many fun and important things about babies and how to keep them safe. Your mom and dad will be pleased with all you've learned.

Remember that you will always need to ask your adult if you may play with your new little brother or sister.

A SPECIAL NOTE TO PARENTS

This book will help your child welcome the new baby. It will encourage interest in the baby and in being a big sister or brother.

The activities are designed to open up family discussions and can be easily adapted to your child's age and abilities. Reading and working in this book together will let your child know that he or she is an important member of the family.

- You can use **Part 1**, *All about me*; **Part 2**, *My family gets ready*; and **Part 3**, *All about babies*, from the time you choose to tell your child of the expected baby until her /his actual arrival.

- As soon as the new baby arrives, your child can go on to **Part 4**, *Welcoming the new baby*.

- The last section, **Part 5**, *We grow up together*, encourages your son or daughter to look forward to the days ahead and to learn more about what having a brother or sister really means.

Many pages are planned just for your child who is age two to five (approximately) to do with your help. Other, more difficult activities may be appropriate for an older child of age six to twelve, but some of them might be modified for a younger child.

For example, "Finding Out About Me," page 20, need not be followed as written, but you will surely want to show and talk about the objects such as baby toys and photos, as it reinforces the child's uniqueness. You may want to pick one or two activities from pages 41 and 42, "I Can Hardly Wait" to do together, but a younger child may not be interested or able to do them all.

When drawing a picture, accept the child's ability level and don't ask for recognizable figures. For example, a drawing might look like a scribble but the addition of a label (given by the child and printed by the adult) of "My Family," will make it meaningful to everyone.

Young children are less able than older children to communicate verbally or to understand. They need to do more activities that require movement and motor skills but these abilities are also just beginning to develop. The following activities especially use manipulative skills and body movements but the child may need lots of adult help.

Page 15, Babies are Special; p. 26, My Booklet; p. 27, Treasure Box; p. 37, I Remember; p. 40, Planning Ahead; p. 41, I Can Hardly Wait; p. 42, Touch Book and Zipper Up; p. 50, Dolly Practice; p. 51, Still Growing; p. 52, Fun Drawing and Dressing a Paper Baby; p. 53, Fun Drawing Me; p. 55, Everywhere We Go; p. 56, Baby Faces; p. 58-61, Songs & Games; p. 64, Your Busy-ness; p. 73-75, Announcements; p. 81, Hand in Hand. Other activities that a younger child may enjoy are on pages 15, 23, 24, 25, 26, 27, 33, 34, 35, 38, 39, 45, 46, 47, 48, 49, 52, 66, 69, 70, 76, 77, 78, 82, 83, 86, 96, 97, 98, 99, 100, 109, 116, 120.

For a young child, you may want to fill in special pages so that the book will be a keepsake for the child as he / she grows older. For example, "Finding Out About Me" on page 20, or page 36, "My Helping Record," may be too difficult now but important to remember in the future.

If your child is age six and up, she / he will probably be able to carry out many activities and complete some of the written parts of the book without your help. You will want to allow your child some independence, of course, but stay involved. Remember, the book is intended to encourage family input and discussions so you will want to either guide the activities or do them with the child.

You play an important role in encouraging your child to take part in these preparation activities. For example, when your child helps by doing a family task, urge him/her to enter it on the "Helping Record," page 36.

TIPS
FOR
PARENTS

1. With any age child, but especially ages 2-5, choose the concepts you want to be sure the child knows and repeat them over and over. For example, just learning the words "in" or "on" are important to following directions. Use the concept often, keeping your sentences short and simple. You might say "Put the paper <u>on</u> the table," and "Look, the book is <u>on</u> the chair."

2. Plan a quiet time every day when you can work on an activity or page from the book or just talk about the changes that are coming.

3. Be patient and ready to answer the same questions again and again. Not only is there a lot to understand, but there is time going by in which to forget the answers!

4. With a 2-5 child, pick a page or activity, read it aloud and talk about it. If there is a written portion, you might ask the child to tell you what to write.

5. With a 6-and-up child, agree on what page or activity he /she will be doing, read through it together and answer questions on how she /he might go about doing it. Some activities may require you steering the child in the right direction.

6. Use positive reinforcement. The child may not do an activity the way you would have done it but praise him or her for the creativity shown.

7. If your child is older and does not seem interested, try doing these as family activities. This may tempt her / him to do more, but demanding his / her participation is not a good idea.

8. There are many ways to expand the use of the book with older children. For example, a child might want to learn to play one of the songs he or she learned (Songs and Games to Share, page 58) on the piano.

PART 1

ALL
ABOUT
ME!

A special baby you know!
I was a baby, too!
Searching for clues about me
My great investigation
Finding out about me
Changing from baby to big kid
I like being bigger!
Brothers and sisters

A special
baby
<u>you</u>
know!

Your mom and dad waited
for a **special baby** to be born.

Do you know who that was?

That baby was
YOU!

I was a baby, too!

My mom and dad were very happy
when I became part of the family.

They named me:

_____

Something special about my name is:

_____

_____

I was born on:

Day_____ Month _____ Year_____

I was the: _____first child _____second child

_____third child or _____ child in the family

ACTIVITY: BABIES ARE SPECIAL!

On a large piece of paper or pasteboard, glue pictures of babies
you cut from magazines. You will find many pictures of babies.
Each one is a special member of a family.

Searching for clues about me

A good investigator:

☆ Starts with a plan ☆ Asks questions
☆ Knows who to ask ☆ Looks carefully

 ## Start with a plan:
THE WHO

WHO are the people who knew you when you were a baby? Write their names below. They are the best people to answer your questions and help you find clues:

Name _____

Name _____

Name _____

Name _____

THE WHATS

WHAT **rooms** in your home might have **clues or objects** that would tell you about you when you were a baby?

Room _____

Room _____

_____

WHAT **places** might have **objects or papers** that have been hidden away?

Place _____

Place _____

Place _____

WHAT **papers or objects** do you think you might find?

_____

_____

_____

Now that your plan is ready, **get started!**

My great investigation

about me

On the last two pages, you made a plan to search for clues about yourself as a baby. Here you can write what you found out.

Date:_____

What I did: _____
_____
_____

What I found out: _____
_____
_____

Date:_____

What I did: _____
_____
_____

What I found out: _____
_____
_____

Date:_____

me

What I did: _____

_____

What I found out: _____

_____

Date:_____

What I did: _____

_____

What I found out: _____

_____

ME?

_____

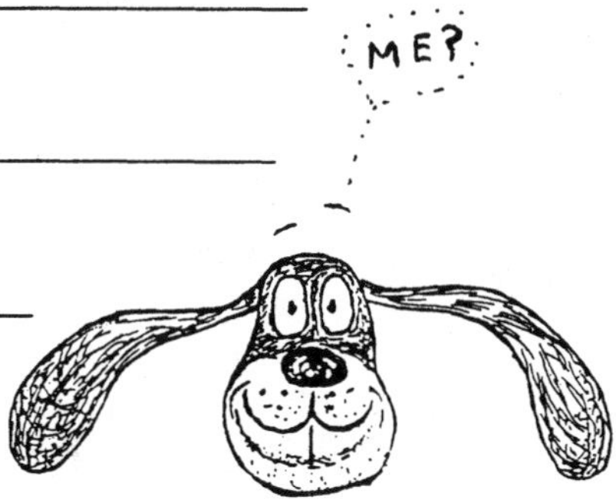

Finding out
about me

Check which items you found:
1. _____ Your Birth Certificate
2. _____ Your favorite toys
3. _____ Your baby pictures
4. _____ Some favorite clothes

1. Did you find your
Birth Certificate?

Here is some information you can find on it:

Length of my footprint: _____ inches

My height: _____ inches

My weight: _____ pounds _____ ounces

Time of birth: _____ (a.m. _____ or p.m. _____ ?)

Doctor's name: _____

Name of the hospital: _____

2. Did you find
your favorite
baby toys?

Here is my list: _____

_____

3. Did you find your baby pictures?

Here are some baby pictures
you can look for:

(Check the ones you found)

____ Me having my first bath

____ Me eating

____ Me with my whole family

____ Me at the hospital

____ Me in my first bed

____ Me sleeping

____ Me with mom

4. Did you find your baby clothes?

Here are some baby clothes I found:

_____

_____

_____

_____

Did you hear your birth day story?

Mom and Dad told me
the story of my birth day.

Their story: _____

_____

_____

_____

This is a story about something funny that happened:

_____

_____

_____

_____

Right after I was born, I had:

_____ some hair _____ a little hair
_____ no hair at all (poor me).

The first day home, I met:

_____

_____

My favorite song was ...

_____

... especially if this person sang it to me:

_____

A toy I liked to sleep with was:

_____

My folks showed me off
when they took me here:

_____

_____

Changing from baby to big kid

Here's a picture taken of me when
I was a very, very new baby:

Glue
your
BABY
picture
here

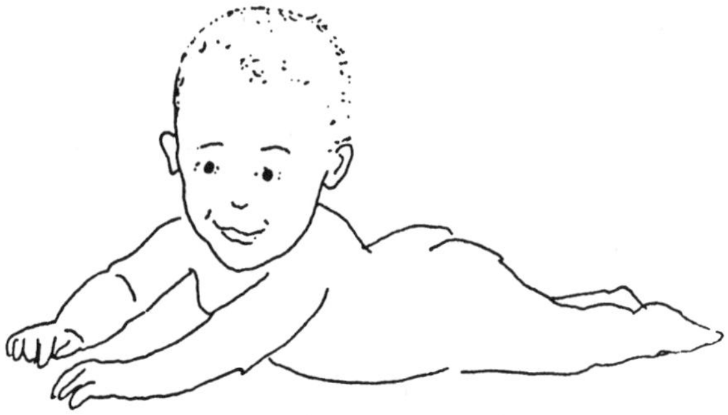

Here's a picture of me TODAY!

Wow! What a difference!

Glue
your
BIG KID
picture
here

About me now:

I am _____ years old.

I am a _____ boy _____ girl.

I have _____ colored eyes
and _____ colored hair.

I live with_____.

A day in my life

Write about what **you** do on an ordinary day. Include the names of friends, pets, places you go, such as preschool, the library, or day care. Tell things you like to do— like color or listen to music.

_____

_____

_____

_____

_____

ACTIVITY: MY BOOKLET

Make up a booklet about **you** right now. To make a booklet, just take three (or more) sheets of paper, fold them in half and staple them along the fold. Put in pictures of **your** favorite neighbors and friends, the place where you live, the park you like to play in, or your favorite toys...anything important in your life. Be sure to write something about them. (**Hint:** This can be a *great gift* for a distant grandparent or other relative.)

From baby to bigger

I have already grown so much!

These are things I **don't** do anymore (For example, you don't wear diapers, suck on a pacifier, or drink from a bottle):

_____

_____

_____

_____

I've grown enough **to do** these things: (**Tell** what I want instead of cry, run fast, help wash dishes, comb my hair, wash my hands, eat a cookie, go to the circus, go fishing or take a pony ride):

_____

_____

_____

I know what I like! These are things I **really like** (carrots, mashed potatoes, chocolate chip cookies, or a teddy bear):

_____

_____

ACTIVITY: TREASURE BOX

Make a Treasure Box to keep your important things in. Get a shoebox or any box with a lid. Cover the box and the lid with paper you like or aluminum foil. Write on the outside: (your name's) Treasure Box. Decorate the box with stickers or drawings. Look for some favorite things to keep in it.

I like being bigger!

I'm blasting off to being a big kid! Here's a countdown of my experiences:

5 Big kid things I have learned to do:
(Tie my shoes? Ride a bike? Get Dressed? Other?)

My list: _____

_____

4 Special places I have been:
(A zoo? Circus? Play group?)

_____

_____

3 Special things I am allowed to do:
(Take lessons? Sleep over?)

_____

_____

2 Special changes I would like when I become a big brother
or big sister: (More allowance? Bigger bed?)

_____

_____

1 A special privilege I am hoping for in the future:
(A later bedtime? A pet?)

_____

_____

Brothers and Sisters

I'm already a **big brother / big sister**.

I have a younger (sister or brother) named
_____, age _____.

Another younger (sister or brother) is named
_____. His or her age is _____.

Others: _____

_____

I'm already a **little sister / little brother**

I have an older (sister or brother) named

_____, age _____.

Another older (sister or brother) is named
_____. His or her age is _____.

Others: _____

_____

PART 2

MY FAMILY
GETS READY

How many noses?
I am ready to help!
My helping record!
Helping with Dump Day!
Things to do to get ready!
I can hardly wait!

Your family
is waiting
for a
special baby again!
♥ You are happy
and excited—
and busy getting ready!

How many noses?

♥ How many people
are in your family?

_____

How many girls? _____

How many boys? _____

How many noses? _____

How many fingers? _____

How many hearts? _____

How many eyes? _____

How many toes? _____

♥ ACTIVITIES: FAMILIES

1/ Collect photos of families you know. Put them all together in
a group on a poster or in an album. Talk about each family —
are they cousins? Friends? 2/ On a large piece of paper or posterboard,
glue pictures of families cut from magazines. Remember that there are
different kinds of families.

♥ I AM
READY
TO HELP!

Your mom is busy doing a very important job.
She is taking care of the baby growing inside
her. She is working so hard at her special job
that she may need extra rest
and she may also need extra help.

BRILLIANT BRAIN: *Good to plan a surprise for mom.* ♥

Your surprise: Fill a box, bag or basket with 14 small gifts (some for her, some for baby). Tell her to open one every day starting about two weeks before the baby might come. For the baby, you can plan a surprise of a small stuffed toy, bib or booties. *Additional ideas:* You can give mom IOU's for washing dishes or watering the garden, or something else you can think of to help.

EAGLE EYES: To see when mom needs help. (Like tying her shoelaces.)

♥ **ESCALATOR VOICE:** To go up loud for playing outside and to go down low when mom is resting.

GRIPPER HANDS: To carry a pillow for mom's back, slippers for her feet, and a glass of milk.

RACING FEET: To run and get whatever mom needs.

♥

MY
HELPING
RECORD

Here is a record of some ways I helped our family

Date   **I helped by doing this:**

----------   --

----------   --

----------   --

----------   --

----------   --

----------   --

----------   --

----------   --

----------   --

----------   --

----------   --

Date   I helped by doing this:

- - - - - - - - - -   -

- - - - - - - - - -   -

- - - - - - - - - -   -

- - - - - - - - - -   -

- - - - - - - - - -   -

- - - - - - - - - -   -

- - - - - - - - - -   -

- - - - - - - - - -   -

ACTIVITIES: "I REMEMBER" GAME

Here is a game to practice following directions. A parent will play it
with you. You can see how well you can listen and do.

*Note to parent: Give your child a simple one-part direction which has to do with
helping the baby. For example, you can say, "Please go to the crib." Then let your
child do the task. Did he or she remember? Be certain to follow up with lots of praise.
Or you can make the remembering a little more complex for an older child by adding
parts: "Please get the baby's teddy bear from the crib and bring it to me." Keep prac-
ticing. When the child is successful with two-part directions, try three. You can do
this over a period of months. Throughout, the child will learn vocabulary
and recognition of items associated with the new sibling.*

This goes here — that goes there!

*Here's another game. You can learn where things go to help the family.
Find out where to put toys, dirty clothes, and trash.*

HELPING
WITH
DUMP DAY!

Your family may be planning a DUMP DAY!
That's a day to get out boxes of baby clothes,
blankets, bottles and other things the baby will
need. On Dump Day, you can help your mom
and dad find your old baby things and help get
them ready for the new baby.

FIND

the first toys the baby will play with,

such as: _____ rattles _____ soft stuffed animals

_____ things that can be squeaked

_____ or things that are made to be chewed

*Help wash them and put them in a special box
or basket. (Maybe you can decorate it.)*

FIND

the clothes the baby will wear

right away, such as:

_____ pajamas with feet _____ undershirts

_____ or little socks

*Help wash and put them away
in the baby's own drawers.*

FIND OUT

what other things your family

must get ready, such as:

_____ putting up the crib

_____ getting out a car seat

_____ cleaning a baby bathtub

_____ or buying diapers

Things to do
to get ready

Help your mom and dad by making a list here.
Check each task off when you have completed it:

DONE

1 _____ ☐

2 _____ ☐

3 _____ ☐

4. _____ ☐

5 _____ ☐

6 _____ ☐

7 _____ ☐

8 _____ ☐

ACTIVITY: PLANNING AHEAD

Plan a walk that you will take with the baby. Put a doll in a stroller
and decide on a fun walk. When you see something pretty
or interesting, hear a bird or a train, show the baby! Here are some places
we will go on our walk:

_____   _____

_____   _____

I CAN HARDLY WAIT!

Five handy things to do while you wait

1 Make a special sign to put up on the day the baby comes home. You could draw a picture of your family on the sign and write, "Welcome to our Family."

After you know the baby's name, you could add:

"We love you, _____

(add the baby's name)

2 Make a sign that says, SHHHHHH—BABY IS SLEEPING. Use cardboard or posterboard and decorate the sign. Put the sign in a place you will be certain to see it when you come in from outside. Turn it over until you need it.

3 Decorate a box or bag to hold some special "Mom and Me" and "Dad and Me" plans. Cut some slips of paper and write one activity you plan to do on each one. You might want, "Bake cookies with Mom," or "Take a walk with Dad." Put all the slips into the box or bag and mark the outside with the instructions to draw one or two slips every week.

4 Stitch, color or paint a picture for the baby's room. (Check an art store for coloring posters.) Before you frame it, sign your name and the date. Hang your gift in the baby's room.

5 Prepare a special gift just for baby. Here are **two projects** you can make with a parent or a grandparent:

BABY BIB

Plan and make a bib for baby to use. Choose a pattern, pick a design, and work together on a cloth or towel bib.

TOUCH BOOK

Collect materials that "feel" different when you touch them (like sandpaper, cotton ball, feather). Some may be soft, smooth, gritty, fluffy, etc. Be sure none are sharp or could harm the baby. Staple or glue pieces of the materials onto paper or cloth, then sew or lace the pages together to make a book. You can use a marker to add words if you want to.

ACTIVITY: ZIPPER UP!

Get out some of baby's clothes, including sleepers and outerwear. Practice buttoning, snapping, and using velcro closures.

Note to parents: If your child is old enough, show him or her how to protect the baby's skin while zipping up clothing. If you have an educational toy that teaches these skills, use it, or dress a doll in baby clothes for more practice.

PART 3

ALL
ABOUT
BABIES

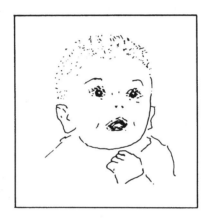

Baby watch   The zoo won't do!
May I?   Growing ... growing!
I'm still growing, too!
Switches!   Everywhere we go
Baby faces   Songs and games to share!
Busy Days
I earned my Baby Ready Certificate

You will be a fun
big sister
or **big brother**.

You will want to find out
the most
important things
about babies!

Baby watch

On the lookout for babies!

Names of some babies I know:

------------------------------   -----------------------------

------------------------------   -----------------------------

If you are watching, you will see babies in many places
you go — the store, bus, park, beach or restaurant.
Write down where you went and
how many babies you counted.

Date	Where I went	How many babies?
Date	Where I went	How many babies?
Date	Where I went	How many babies?
Date	Where I went	How many babies?
Date	Where I went	How many babies?

When you see a baby, guess whether he or she is:

Less than 1 year: --- can't sit up or move around at all --- maybe can sit up
and crawl, but not walk --- mostly drinks milk and maybe
eats some baby food

More than 1 year: --- can WALK --- can say "bye-bye" or "Da-Da" or
more words --- can drink from a cup and eat little pieces of real food

THE ZOO WON'T DO!

Have you ever seen a baby animal
with its mother?
It's fun to watch how the mother
cares for her baby.

But the best way to learn
about taking care of a baby brother or sister
is to watch a human mother with her family.

The pictures here will show you
some animal mothers and babies.
You can visit a human mother and baby
or ask your adult to help you learn
about baby care.

**Then write what
you found out!**

**A mother
kangaroo**

holds
her baby
like **this**

**THE ZOO
WON'T
DO!**

I learned to hold
a baby like this:

A mother cat

carries
her baby
like this

THE ZOO
WON'T DO!

I learned
to carry
a baby this way:

A baby panda bear

eats
this
way

**THE ZOO
WON'T DO!**

I learned that
a baby
eats this way:

A baby opossum
sleeps
like this:

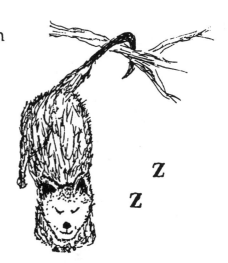

Z

Z

THE ZOO WON'T DO!

I learned that a baby
sleeps like this:

♥ ACTIVITY: DOLLY PRACTICE

Ask your mom or dad to help you practice baby care
with a baby doll. You can learn lifting, carrying, holding,
burping, feeding, playing, sleeping positions,
dressing, washing, and lots more.

MAY I?

 Mom and Dad need me
to follow a few rules:

___ Pick up the baby when Mom or Dad say it's OK,
if I do it the way they tell me to do it.

___ Touch the baby very gently with one finger.

___ Give the baby food or drinks
made just for babies (not mine).

___ Give the baby his or her own
special toys (not mine).

I realize I am strong, so I must be careful with
my new baby brother or baby sister.

♡ O T H E R   R U L E S

- -

- -

- -

- -

- -

Growing... growing!

It may not seem like babies get bigger very fast,
but they are growing all the time.
While you are waiting for the baby,
try growing some outside flowers or indoor plants.

What do flowers or plants
need to grow?

What do babies
need to grow?

Fun drawing & dressing a paper baby

On a large piece of butcher paper or posterboard, trace a doll or draw a
realistic-sized baby shape. The adult can draw in the facial features and the
child can color the hair to match his or her own baby pictures. Next, get out
one of the child's baby outfits, one for the new baby, or just use a picture of
one, and draw the outline of the clothes. Let the child color in the clothes on
the " baby " to match the outfit.

I'm still growing, too!

THEN

Check back on **Page 20** to fill
in your sizes when you were born

NOW

Ask an adult to help you
check your sizes today

Birth Date

‗‗‗‗‗‗‗‗‗‗‗‗‗‗‗‗‗‗

Today's Date

‗‗‗‗‗‗‗‗‗‗‗‗‗‗‗‗‗‗

Length of my footprint:
_____ inches

My height: _____ inches

My weight:
_____ pounds _____ ounces

Length of my footprint:
_____ inches

My height: _____ inches

My weight:
_____ pounds _____ ounces

Fun drawing me — twice!

Adults: **1/** Lay a large piece of butcher paper, posterboard or paper
from a roll on the floor. Have the child lie on it while you trace his or her outline. Help the child make the facial features and choose either the outfit he
or she is wearing or bring out a different one. Draw in the clothes and let the
child color or paint them.

2/ Make a poster of the child. Use pictures of different ages
to show growth. Full-length photos would be great!
Be sure to include a newborn picture and a recent picture.

♥ ♥ ♥ ♥ ♥ ♥ ♥ ♥ ♥ ♥ ♥ ♥ SWITCHES! ♥ ♥ ♥

Lots of fun **switches** may be going on soon. Will you switch bedrooms with the new baby? Will you switch from your usual seat in the car to a different place when the baby's car seat goes in? When baby starts to sit in a high chair, will you switch places at the table?

Here is a place to keep track of those **switches** you see, both before and after the new baby comes:

Date   Switch!

- - - - - - - -   -

- - - - - - - -   -

- - - - - - - -   -

- - - - - - - -   -

- - - - - - - -   -

- - - - - - - -   -

- - - - - - - -   -

- - - - - - - -   -

- - - - - - - -   -

- - - - - - - -   -

EVERYWHERE WE GO

Wherever you are, look for things a baby might use at that place. Does the grocery store have a special seat in the shopping cart for a small baby? Do some of the carts have a strap for an older baby? Does the restaurant you are at have high chairs or booster seats to use? Is there a special place in the restroom to change a baby's diaper? Find the baby food at the grocery store. Would you like to buy a jar and taste it?

Make a list of places you go and what you see there for babies:

Place	Something the baby might use
- - - - - - - - - - - - - - -	- -
- - - - - - - - - - - - - - -	- -
- - - - - - - - - - - - - - -	- -
- - - - - - - - - - - - - - -	- -
- - - - - - - - - - - - - - -	- -
- - - - - - - - - - - - -	- -

What are some other places you will take the baby? To day care? Church? Nursery? Grandparents' home? Ask your mom or dad to show you where the baby will be at when he or she is at those places. Find out where the baby will sleep at home.

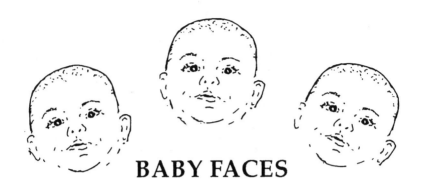

BABY FACES

Here are some fun activities to do
WITH YOUR HANDS

1. Draw the outline of an imaginary baby's head with a washable marker or fingerpaint on finger-painting paper, waxed paper, or just a smooth surface.

With fingerpaints or a washable marker, add eyes, ears, nose, mouth, and hair to your drawing. Or, with help from an adult, you can design the baby's face using spaghetti hair, macaroni mouth, frosting cheeks, and candy eyes.

Use cooked and cooled oatmeal, whipped cream, or applesauce to paint a picture of a baby who is a messy eater.

Do your parents or grandparents have a photograph of you with food on your face when you were a baby? Ask to see it! Or ask if you can look in a mirror with some of the oatmeal, whipped cream, or sauce
on *your face!*

2. Draw a *large* picture of a baby face on paper or posterboard. Have an adult help you draw several thick, dark lines on the picture and cut it apart into big pieces to make a puzzle. Mix up the pieces and put the puzzle back together again.

**See if others can do
the puzzle!**

3. Decorate round cookies with candies to make a baby's face.

**And without
your hands...**

4. Sit in front of a mirror and try to make faces like you think a baby might make, such as
- crying
- angry
- sleepy
- or surprised.

5. Get a partner (a parent, grandparent, brother, sister or friend) and sit in front of a mirror so you can see each other and yourselves at the same time.

- Make **funny faces** at each other
- Try to make the **same face** at the **same time**
- Try to make a face **like the other is making**

Songs and games to share

Babies love it when you **sing** to them and **play** baby **games** with them. Ask your mom, dad, and grandparents to teach you their favorite **songs** and **games** for babies. You can also ask friends and neighbors or look in books for ideas.

 Here are some of the **fun songs** I learned to sing for the baby:

Name of the song I learned: _

I learned it from: _

Words of the song:

_ _

_ _

_ _

_ _

_ _

_ _

_ _

Name of the song I learned: _____

I learned it from: _____

☆ Words of the song:

_____

_____

_____

_____

_____

_____

Name of the song I learned: _____

I learned it from: _____

Words of the song: ☆

_____

_____

_____

_____

_____

_____

Fun games!

Do you know "This Little Piggy" and "Peek-A-Boo?"
Here are some of the **games** I learned
to play with the baby:

Name of game I learned: _____

I learned it from: _____

How to play the game:

_____

_____

_____

_____

_____

_____

_____

_____

Name of game I learned: _____

I learned it from: _____

How to play the game:

_____

_____

_____

_____

_____

_____

Name of game I learned: _____

I learned it from: _____

How to play the game:

_____

_____

_____

_____

Dog-gone!

_____

BUSY DAYS

You are ready for the baby to come

You are excited about enjoying your new sister or brother. Here are a few more things you should know about the busy days after the baby comes:

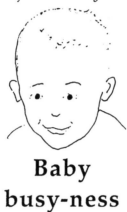

Baby
busy-ness

___ The baby may need to go to the doctor's office or hospital for tests or check-ups. There are some special tests that every baby needs. Your parents want to be sure that the baby is healthy.

___ The baby will sleep and eat, sleep and eat, and then sleep and eat again! That's because sleeping and eating are just about all that newborn babies do.

___ The baby will cry in between eating and sleeping. You might think that something is wrong — or that your mom and dad are not trying hard enough, but the baby is probably only crying about as much as any other baby cries. And there are reasons for all that crying!

Mom & Dad
busy-ness

___Your mom will need extra rest. She is tired from her job of caring for the baby. She might have been awake taking care of the baby while you were asleep.

___Your dad may be able to stay home from work for a day or two after the baby arrives. He will want to help with the baby, but he will probably have some extra time to play with you, too!

Family
& friends
busy-ness

___ People will come to visit. Your family and friends are just as excited about the new baby as you are! Some will come for a short visit; some may stay longer.

___ People will call on the telephone to talk, especially family members who do not live nearby.

Your busy-ness: CAMERA FRENZY

You will have to pose for lots and lots of pictures!
You will think of things to do with all those pictures:

Ask your mom or dad to take a
picture of you with the new baby
together every three months.

Glue the first one in your book
now to get started.

Send some pictures
to relatives
who live far away.

Make a scrapbook that will be
for any pictures of you
with your new brother or sister.

Make a frame with paper or craft materials.
Put a picture of yourself in the frame
and place it in the baby's room.

You will start doing all the things
you have learned — helping your family
and helping with the baby.

Other
busy-ness
for me

☆ Make a list of things you can do for the baby.
Both you and your parents can think of ideas

1 _____

2 _____

3 _____

4 _____

5 _____

6 _____

7 _____

8 _____

9 _____

10 _____

I earned my Baby-Ready Certificate

I am now Baby-Ready

♥ I practiced baby care

♥ I helped my family get ready

♥ I learned songs
and games for babies

♥ I promise to love and protect
the new baby in our family

_____

Signature

_____

Date

PART 4

WELCOMING THE NEW BABY!

I see the new baby!   Isn't that a cute baby?

I am happy to announce!   Do we look alike?

Was I ever that little?   Hand in hand

What can baby do?   Baby talk   Just call on me!

My family helping record   How baby learns

What will baby do all day?   My Day

How we can play together   I talk to baby

What are they talking about?

My record of activities with baby

The new baby is special

You have
a new
baby sister
or
baby brother!

You will want
to get to know
the new baby
right away.

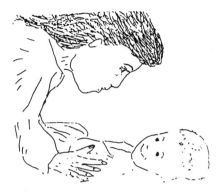

I SEE THE NEW BABY!

And here is my important record

♥ Our family's **new baby** was born on:

_____

Day of the week

_____

Month   Day   Year

♥ The baby's **full name** is:

_____

First name

_____

Middle name

_____

Last name

The baby weighs:

--------------------   --------------------
Pounds   Ounces

That is (_____ more) or (_____ less)
than I weighed when I was born.

♥ I weighed:

--------------------   --------------------
Pounds   Ounces

The baby's eyes are this color: ♥

I first heard the news of baby's birth
from this person:

When the baby came, I was at this location:

♥ I was busy doing this:

♥ I first saw the baby on this date:

At this location:

♥ I first held the baby on this date:

At this location:

My feelings: ♥

How many noses now?

How many boys? _____ How many girls? _____

How many noses? _____ How many ears? _____

How many fingers? _____ How many toes? _____

How many eyes? _____

How many loving hearts? _____

**How many people
are in your family now?** _____

ISN'T THAT A CUTE BABY?

Everybody loves babies! If you listen carefully, you will hear family and friends say many of the same things over and over when they see the new baby.

Have you heard someone say these things?

"What an adorable baby!"   *"The baby looks just like..."*
"How tiny!"   *"You must be so proud!"*

Your project is a fun one: Keep a list of the things people say about your new baby brother or sister. Write some of these sayings below. When he or she is older, you can show them to your brother or sister.

1 _____

2 _____

3 _____

4 _____

5 _____

I AM HAPPY TO ANNOUNCE!

Now that the baby has arrived...

☆ You can put up the

W E L C O M E   H O M E

sign

you made

(Activity number 1 on page 41)

You can make and send or deliver
your own announcements to neighbors
or friends at school, day care, church,
play group or other places.

You'll find two ideas

on the next pages

☆ A SPECIAL ANNOUNCEMENT

1/ Use a paper plate 2/ Draw a face with a marker

3/ Add hair color and eye color to match baby's

4/ Add a pink hairbow on the top for a girl. Add a blue bow tie on the bottom for a boy.

5/ Write the announcement on the other side:

ANNOUNCING
my new
baby brother (or baby sister)

His or her name:_____

The date he or she was born:_____

His or her weight:_____

Signed_____
His proud sister (or brother)

Give your special announcement to your friends!

⭐ A BABY RATTLE ANNOUNCEMENT WITH A TREAT!

1/ Use two paper nut cups.

2/ Poke two holes in each cup.

3/ Thread a piece of curling ribbon through the holes. Tie the ribbon on the inside of the cups.

4/ Fill one cup with small candies.

5/ Write an announcement. Roll it up and put it inside:

I'M A BIG SISTER
(or a Big Brother)

The baby's name: _____

Date of birth: _____

Signed (your name) _____

Big Brother (or Big Sister)

6/ Glue the rims of the two cups together.

7/ Treat your friends to a baby rattle announcement.

Do we look alike?

Here is one of the first pictures
taken of the baby:

I think baby looks like me
because we have the same:

_____ kind of nose   _____ color of eyes

_____ kind of hair   _____ beautiful smile!

Together:

(Baby's name) _____

and me on this date: _____

I am proud to have a baby _____.

(brother or sister)

(Baby's name) _____

is lucky to have me for a big

_____

(sister or brother)

Was I ever that little?

♥ You can discover **the wonder** of a brand-new baby:

Look at the baby's feet and toes.
Are they as big as yours? ____ Yes ____ No

Count the toes.
How many are there? _____

Does the baby have toenails?
____ Yes ____ Not yet

How does baby's skin feel?
Is it smooth or rough? _____
What color is it? _____

Stroke the baby's skin gently.
Does the baby like to be touched?
____ Yes ____ No

Look at the baby's hands and fingers.
Have baby's fingernails been cut yet?
____ Yes ____ No

When I put my finger inside baby's hand,
this happens:

_____

_____

When I touch one of baby's cheeks, this happens:

_____

_____

Very gently touch the baby's hair.
Is it soft? ___ Yes ___ No

Ask your mom or dad why it is so important
to be careful of baby's head.

Look at the baby's lips.
Do baby's lips move even when he or she is not eating?
___ Yes ___ No

Can you see bumps where baby's teeth will be?
___ Yes ___ No

Does the baby have eyelashes?
____ Yes ____ Not yet

Are they long or short? _____

♥

Does baby open his or her eyes very often?
____ Yes ____ No

What sounds does baby make?

_____

_____

_____

Does the baby cry softly _____ or loudly _____?

Does the baby make a sound when eating?
____ Yes ____ No

What sound?_____

When I gently touch one of baby's ears,
this happens:

_____

When baby hears a sudden sound,
this happens:

_____

When I gently touch the baby's lips,
this happens:

_____

What fun babies are!

Hand in hand

Trace your hand below. Now trace the baby's hand inside it with a different color.
Write your names inside the drawings.

Date:_____

What can baby do?

You may be surprised when you watch your
new brother or sister and see
how many things he or she can do already.

1. Sit right next to the baby. Read each line on the
chart on the next page and decide whether you can
do it. You can even try to do each one right now!

If you can, put an X under "I Can."

2. Think about whether the baby can do the same
thing. Your mom or dad can help you remember
and decide what you have already seen baby do.

If baby can, put an X on the line under "Baby Can."

At the bottom of the chart, you can add
ideas you think of.

Date _____

	I CAN	BABY CAN
	Age _____	Age _____
Hear noises	_____	_____
See	_____	_____
Taste	_____	_____
Smell	_____	_____
Feel	_____	_____
Talk	_____	_____
Cry	_____	_____
Breathe	_____	_____
Kick legs	_____	_____
Wave arms	_____	_____
Suck thumb	_____	_____
Blink	_____	_____
Understand	_____	_____
Hum	_____	_____
Sing	_____	_____
Whistle	_____	_____
Chew	_____	_____
Swallow	_____	_____
Walk	_____	_____
Crawl	_____	_____

OTHER IDEAS

_____ _____ _____

_____ _____ _____

_____ _____ _____

BABY TALK o o

How does your baby brother or sister
"talk" to you? When **you** need something,
you can use words to tell your mom or dad,
but what can the baby do?

When you hear the baby crying, you get to play
a game. You can try to **guess** what the baby
is telling you. Your mom and dad played this
game when you were a baby, too—so they will
probably guess faster.

Is the baby saying:

I'm hungry

I'm sleepy

I'm cold

I need to burp

I feel uncomfortable

I am too hot

Write
your guesses
on the next page

M M M E E E E E E

What baby is saying

Date	My guess	Check here if you were right
- - - - - - -	- -	- - - - - -
- - - - - - -	- -	- - - - - -
- - - - - - -	- -	- - - - - -
- - - - - - -	- -	- - - - - -
- - - - - - -	- -	- - - - - -
- - - - - - -	- -	- - - - - -
- - - - - - -	- -	- - - - - -
- - - - - - -	- -	- - - - - -
- - - - - - -	- -	- - - - - -
- - - - - - -	- -	- - - - - -
- - - - - - -	- -	- - - - - -

**Can you guess
what baby
is telling you?**

Just call on me!

Here is a list of jobs that I can do to help the whole family

I can:

___ Pick up toys

___ Take messages

___ Bring in the mail or paper

___ Make lists

___ Fold laundry and put it away

___ Report on the baby

___ Go get whatever someone needs

More ideas from Mom and Dad

- -

- -

I can do these things just for the baby

___ Wind up a music box

___ Start a mobile

___ Take off baby's shoes and socks

___ Talk or sing

___ Bring the bottle or pacifier

___ Wind up the baby swing

___ Just be around

More ideas

(from Mom and Dad)

- -

- -

- -

 # My family
helping
record

Here is a record of some ways
I helped our family:

Date	I helped by doing this
- - - - - - - - - - -	- -
- - - - - - - - - - -	- -
- - - - - - - - - - -	- -
- - - - - - - - - - -	- -
- - - - - - - - - - -	- -
- - - - - - - - - - -	- -
- - - - - - - - - - -	- -
- - - - - - - - - - -	- -
- - - - - - - - - - -	- -
- - - - - - - - - - -	- -
- - - - - - - - - - -	- -

Date

I helped by doing this

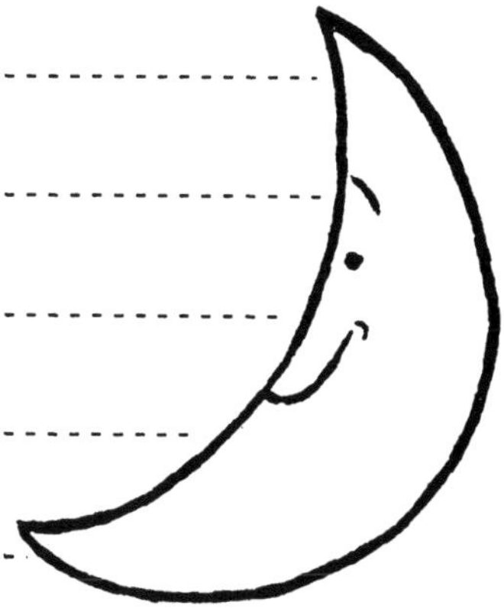

How baby learns

How do **you learn** about the world? You see, smell, hear, taste and touch to find out about things. You can also learn by **asking other people** about their favorite smells, sounds, tastes, and things to touch. You can guess about baby's favorite things, too.

♥ **P E R S O N ' S   N A M E**

- -

His or her favorite:

Smell _____

Sound _____

Taste _____

Touch_____

♥ PERSON'S NAME

His or her favorite:

Smell _____

Sound _____

Taste _____

Touch_____

♥ PERSON'S NAME

His or her favorite:

Smell _____

Sound _____

Taste _____

Touch_____

♥   P E R S O N ' S   N A M E

His or her favorite:

Smell _____

Sound _____

Taste _____

Touch_____

M Y N A M E

My favorite:

Smell _____

Sound _____

Taste _____

Touch_____

♥

I think
baby
would pick
these favorites:

♥ Smell

_____

♥ Sound

_____

♥ Taste

_____

♥ Touch

_____

What will baby do all day?

Here is a place to record **one day** of baby's life. It will be fun to tell someone who wasn't there what the baby did all day on _____!

(date)

Here is a way to keep track:

Every time the baby takes a nap,
put an X in this box.

Every time the baby gets a bath,
put an X in this box.

Every time the baby has a visitor,
put an X in this box.

Every time the baby changes clothes,
put an X in this box.

Every time the baby changes diapers,
put an X in this box.

Every time the baby stays awake a while,
put an X in this box.

Today, the baby had this many:

Naps _____   Changes of clothes _____

Baths _____   Diaper changes _____

Visitors _____   "Awake" times _____

MY DAY

Here's how I spent one whole day

Name _____ Date _____

How we can play together

PLAYGROUND RULES

Make sure either mom or dad tells you it's OK to play with baby. Only play games that are safe for the baby.

Baby loves to see your face, so stay very close where he or she can see you.

If baby keeps watching you, he or she is having fun.

Baby loves to play the same game again and again.

You can play when the baby is in a seat, swing, a lap, on a bed, or on a blanket on the floor.

If baby starts to cry, he or she may need to rest a moment. He or she won't want to play if it is time to eat or sleep.

PLAYGROUND FUN

Say a rhyme and
do motions
with your hands
and with
the baby's hands.

Show the baby something bright and moving,
like a scarf, a pennant, a child's mobile,
or anything else your parents approve.
Keep it close to the baby so he or she can see it.
Let the baby touch what you are holding,
unless it could hurt the baby.

Show the baby a rattle and shake it.
Then move slowly around the room
while you shake the rattle
and say the baby's name.

Sing a song and clap or do
hand motions. Move
the baby's hands
and feet while you sing.

 **Play one of the baby games
you have learned (pages 60 - 61).**

I talk to baby

When?

Anytime the baby is awake
and listening to you.

Where?

Sitting next to the baby.
Holding the baby.

 ## Why?

So the baby can learn to talk
when he or she is bigger.
So the baby will learn
to know your voice.
So the baby
will feel loved.

What?

You can tell the baby about things that are happening
around him or her. Like this:

"I just saw the puppy run by.
Did you see the puppy run by?
He was running fast!"

Write something you said here

- -

- -

- -

- -

You can tell the baby about something
you are showing him or her, like this:

"Here is your blue rattle. It has yellow flowers
on it and it makes a noise when I shake it."

Write something you said here

- -

- -

- -

- -

You can talk about the baby.
Use the baby's name over and over
like this:

"Look at Katy's long fingers!
They are pretty fingers, Katy.
I like to see Katy's pretty fingers."

Write something you said here

- -

- -

- -

- -

- -

If you get tired of thinking
of things to talk about,
don't forget the baby
loves to hear
Y OU
sing or hum
a song!

What are they talking about?

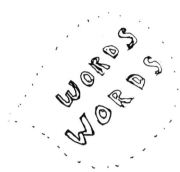

Have you heard these words?

pediatrician

formula

gums

What they mean:

A *pediatrician* is a doctor just for babies and kids.

Formula is a special baby milk.

Gums are part of the mouth where baby's teeth grow (and so do yours).

Have you heard
W O R D S
that you don't know?

They are probably words about babies
and baby things. You can write the words here
and ask an adult what they mean.

Word: **What it means:**

- - - - - - - - - - - - - - - -   -

- - - - - - - - - - - - - - - -   -

- - - - - - - - - - - - - - - -   -

- - - - - - - - - - - - - - - -   -

- - - - - - - - - - - - - - - -   -

- - - - - - - - - - - - - - - -   -

- - - - - - - - - - - - - - - -   -

- - - - - - - - - - - - - - - -   -

- - - - - - - - - - - - - - - -   -

- - - - - - - - - - - - - - - -   -

- - - - - - - - - - - - - - - -   - - - - - - - - - - - - - - - - - - -

My record of activities with BABY

Here is a list of some fun things

_____

(baby's name)

and I did together

Date:  **What we did:**

- - - - - - - - - -   -

- - - - - - - - - -   -

- - - - - - - - - -   -

- - - - - - - - - -   -

- - - - - - - - - -   -

- - - - - - - - -   -

- - - - - - - - - -   -

Dog-gone!

- - - - - - - - - -   -

- - - - - - - - - -   - - - - - - - - - - - - - - - - - - -

Date: **What we did:**

ACTIVITY

Look back at page 40 to see a walk you planned.
Look back at pages 58 - 61 for songs to sing and games you can play.

Have you done them yet?

The new baby is SPECIAL

Today my new

baby _____

(sister - brother)

is _____ days old.

(number)

It seems like baby and I
have had our pictures taken
at least

_____ times.

So far my favorite thing to do with baby is

_____

I like helping by

_____

_____

I asked everyone in the family to tell something about the baby in only
O N E   W O R D

Here is what they told me:

Mom

_____

Dad

_____

Name _____ word _____
Name _____ word _____
Name _____ word _____

And here is what I think
is the
B E S T   W O R D
that tells about baby

_____

PART 5

☆ WE GROW UP TOGETHER!

Teaching baby

I am older, baby is younger

Do you want to be...   Growing up special

Growing up friends!

Other brothers and sisters

Baby's firsts!   Baby's learning record

I love you

⭐ **Your new baby brother or sister**
is growing and learning quickly.
You will see how much fun
you can have together.

How can
you tell
if the baby
is learning?

⭐ You may see that the baby stays awake
more during the day.

The baby may stop crying more quickly
when he or she is picked up or fed.

When you talk, the baby may make
sounds back at you. ⭐

TEACHING BABY

Make a list of things you will help teach
the baby when he or she is old enough.
Here are some ideas: how to blow a kiss,
how to count to ten, and how to make
animal sounds.

1 _____

2 _____

3 _____

4 _____

5 _____

6 _____

7 _____

8 _____

9 _____

10 _____

I am OLDER, baby is YOUNGER

Have you been wondering **how old** you will be when your baby brother or sister has his or her first birthday? Here is a chart that is fun to do and that will show you your age and the baby's age for the next five years. On the first line, under *Me*, put your age right now. Finish the chart with your mom's or dad's help. When you read across each line you can see the **baby's age** and **your age** at the same time.

Baby	Me
Newborn	_____
1/2 year	_____
1 year	_____
1 1/2 year	_____
2 years	_____
2 1/2 years	_____
3 years	_____
3 1/2 years	_____
4 years	_____
4 1/2 years	_____
5 years	_____

Do you want to be...

Big brothers and big sisters
have chances to do **different jobs**
as they grow up.

Maybe you will be:

—a baby sitter

—a playmate

—a teacher

—a cheerleader
(encourage baby's learning)

—a helper

—a leader
(put your seatbelt on)

Ideas (yours or your parents')
on other jobs you can do

GROWING UP SPECIAL

As you and your new sister or brother get bigger
and bigger, what do you think will be **special**
about being **kids together** in the same family?
Will it be special because you can plan surprises
for mom and dad together? Or because you
will have someone to play with, even on vacation?
Here's a place to write what you think:

**I think growing up
with a new sister or brother
will be special because:**

 # GROWING UP FRIENDS!

Most moms and dads wish that their children
will be good friends. They may have ideas about how
brothers and sisters get along. Ask your mom
and dad what they wish for their kids as they grow up.
You can write what they say here.

♥ DAD

- -

- -

- -

- -

- -

♥ MOM

- -

- -

- -

- -

- -

Other brothers and sisters

Ask some family members or friends
to remember something about growing up
with their brother or sister. Some might remember
trips the family took, walking to school
together or sharing a room.

♥ **Name** _____

His or her favorite remembrance about **growing up**

_____

A favorite **memory** when they played together
(playing a game, swimming, sledding)

_____

What he or she said was the **best thing** about
having a sister or brother

_____
_____

♥ **Name** _____

His or her favorite remembrance about **growing up**

_____

A favorite **memory** when they played together
(playing a game, swimming, sledding)

_____

What he or she said was the **best thing**
about having a sister or brother

_____

♥ **Name** _____

His or her favorite remembrance about **growing up**

_____

A favorite **memory** when they played together
(playing a game, swimming, sledding)

_____

What he or she said was the **best thing**
about having a sister or brother

_____

_____

BABY'S FIRSTS!

You probably can't remember the first time
you ate ice cream. But your parents can tell you
about the surprised look on your face when you felt
the cold and tasted the sweetness. You will have
the fun of seeing your new baby brother or sister
find out about the world. Be watching for
Baby's Firsts and record them here. Have fun
—but remember some may not happen right away.

Baby's first ice cream   Date _____

What happened _____

_____

Baby's first popsicle   Date _____

What happened _____

_____

Baby's first snow angel   Date_____

What happened _____
_____

Baby's first clapping   Date _____

What happened _____

_____

Baby's first somersault   Date _____

What happened _____

_____

Baby twirls around   Date _____

What happened _____

_____

Baby's first trip down a slide   Date _____

What happened _____
_____

**Baby's first motorboat
sound with mouth**   Date _____

What happened _____

_____

Baby sees soap bubbles   Date _____

What happened _____

_____

Baby's first trike ride   Date _____

What happened _____

_____

**Baby's first time
to say MY NAME**   Date _____

What happened _____

_____

_____

_____

BABY'S LEARNING RECORD

These are some of the important things baby has learned already:

Date	☆	Baby learned
- - - - - - - - -		- -
- - - - - - - - -		- -
- - - - - - - - -		- -
- - - - - - - - -		- -
- - - - - - - - -		- -
- - - - - - - - -		- -
- - - - - - - - -		- -
- - - - - - - - -		- -
- - - - - - - - -		- -
- - - - - - - - -		- -

I
LOVE
YOU

A special letter
to baby

Dear _____

(baby's name)

♡ It was a **special day** for all of us
when you joined our family.
I have been helping take care of you
and I am excited that you will grow
bigger and bigger
so I can play with you more and more.
When you are older, I will tell you
about when you were a baby
and about the things we did together.
But mostly I will tell you how much
we have always loved you.

Love,

My name _____

Date _____

♡